STEP INSIDE!

Cataloging Information

Ham, Catherine.
   Step inside! : a look inside animal homes /Catherine Ham
      32 p. : col. ill. ; 20 cm.
   Includes index (p.).
   Summary: Uses verse and photographs to explore homes and home-related
behavior in animals. Includes a range of taxa, including mammals, amphibians,
birds, reptiles, fish, molluscs, insects, and spiders,

   LC: QL 756 .H35 2012
   Dewey: 591.56
   ISBN-13: 978-0-9832014-2-7 (alk. paper)
      Animals—Habitations—Juvenile literature

Cover Design: Stewart Pack
Art Director: Celia Naranjo
Copy Editor: Tina Miller
Photo Research: Dawn Cusick
Production Assistance: Jackie Kerr

10 9 8 7 6 5 4 3 2 1

First edition

Published by EarlyLight Books, Inc.
1436 Dellwood Road
Waynesville, NC 28786

Text Copyright 2012 Catherine Ham

To Julia . . .

ISBN-13: 978-0-9832014-2-7

STEP INSIDE!

A Look Inside Animal Homes

Catherine Ham

EarlyLight Books

WAYNESVILLE, NORTH CAROLINA, USA

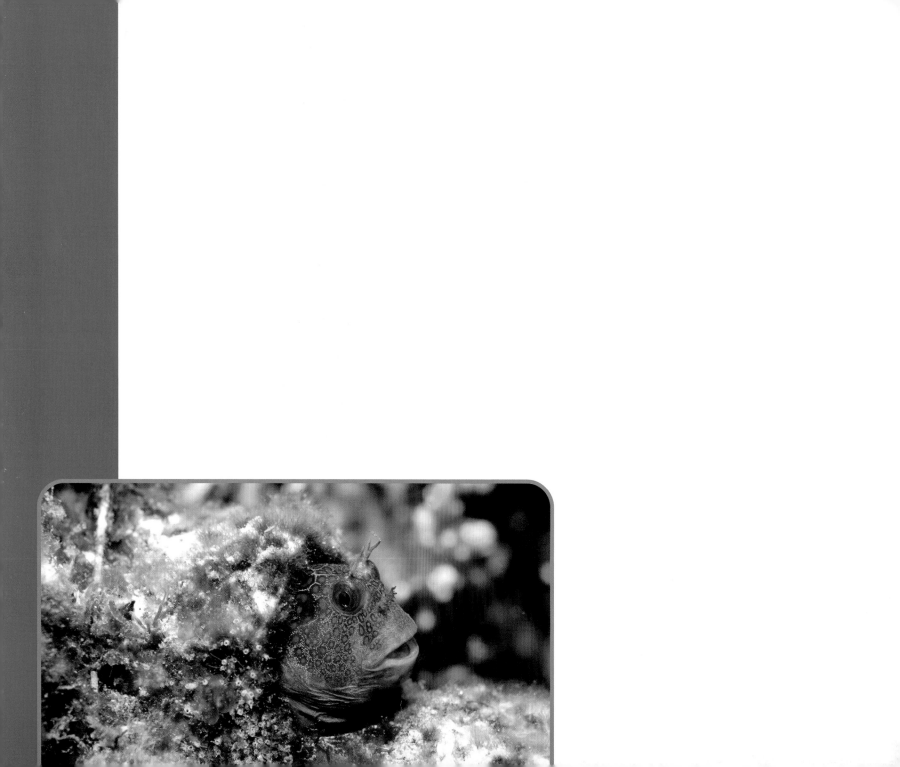

STEP INSIDE!

Which home would you use
If you had to choose?

A hole in a tree
Or one deep in the ground?
A reef in the sea?
Or a tall termite mound?

A home on your back?
A dwelling of sticks?
But none of these creatures
Builds his house of bricks

SAFE & SOUND

Female wasps lay eggs in burrows
Which they dig swiftly into sand
They stock these up with insects
Baby food that's sort of canned

Mother wasps are very caring
Keep the tunnels sealed up tight
Some like their homes so much
They keep on using the same site

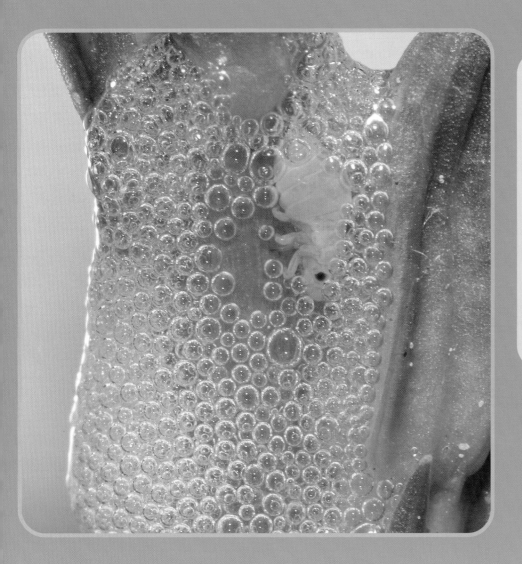

Would it be a lot of trouble
If your home was in a bubble?
This spittlebug thinks not
It's the only house he's got

This froth that he spits out
What's THAT all about?
It keeps him from the eye
Of predators passing by

BUBBLE WRAP

DINNER?

If I were to ask you
Where do spiders live?
IN WEBS! would be the answer
That you'd most likely give

What if I were to tell you
That some spiders have a door?
That they live inside a burrow
Where they even have a floor?
That they never spin a web
But they spin a hinge of silk
So they can easily open
The trapdoor they have built

This crafty door is hidden
By bits of plant and soil
Our spider lies in wait
To catch some insect in his coil

Do you know the story of the 3 little pigs
Who built houses of straw, of sticks, of bricks?
These ants build nests entirely out of leaves
By weaving living leaves together
With the silk that they squeeze
Very gently from ant larvae
High up in the trees

The nests grow to be enormous
These ants toil their whole lives long
You see them here work sharing
As they set about repairing
Their home, to keep it strong

LEAF LIVING

TERMITE HOMES

Pity the poor termite
Who's thought of as a pest
For he likes to feed on rotting wood
But as Nature's cleaner
He's among the very best

Termites live in colonies
They build a cosy nest
From wood, from mud, from spit
Worker termites never rest

The home is usually underground
With a maze of rooms and tunnels
As it grows, it makes a mound
Filled with fresh-air funnels

Where termites live a life
That Man does not disturb
They build amazing homes
Which are truly quite superb!

CAT ON A HOT THIN ROOF

ROOMS WITH A VIEW

Mongoose families are frequently found
Living in a termite mound
They choose an old abandoned nest
From the top the view's the best
From the top, safe and sound
They see the ground from all around

HELLO!

These fat and furry creatures
Have close-knit family ties
They burrow deep in colonies
Which can reach enormous size

They line their homes with grass
To keep them warm and snug
They mostly feed on plants
With now and then, a bug

They have a special bark
To warn of danger drawing near
They escape into their tunnels
Which have doorways, front and rear

All these little mounds
That you see above the ground
Are signs that moles are living there
Safe and sound

In their maze of tunnels
They have pantries to store food
The females burrow out a den
To raise their furry brood

They don't really need to see
So moles are mostly blind
But that doesn't stop them
Catching every bug they find!

HOME GROUND

SLUMBER PARTY!

Take a look...
What do you see?
Hard at first to tell
A jumbled heap
Of sleeping bats
In a corner
Where they dwell

Bats don't build nests
But find themselves
A clean and cosy place
Under eaves, in a cave
Holes in trees are a fave
Quiet spots, dark and safe
Home inside their roosting space

HOME, SWEET HOME

Peeping from her comfy house
Inside a piece of wood
Could be this little field mouse
Thinks her life is very good

Her eyes and ears are huge
Which help her hunt at night
Seeds, berries, bugs and worms
All please her appetite!

A grazing herd of elephants
On Africa's vast plains
Acacia trees for shelter
Long sweet grasses after rains

Great wide open spaces
Free to move around
Summer living's easy
When this is your home ground

A HOME TO ROAM

Four bumps on their heads
Gave warthogs their name
They roam, grazing in groups
On the African plain

KEEP OUT!

They reverse into their dens
Always staying on their guard
If something comes to attack
They'll fight back very hard

Warthogs love a mudbath
It keeps them cool and clean
They'll let a mongoose pick off ticks...
A useful mobile canteen!

PARK & HIDE

These slow moving reptiles
Vary greatly in size
Some species are enormous
Some are tiny little guys

They lay their eggs in nests
To protect them from attack
When the hatchlings emerge
Their lifelong home is on their back

Beavers are busy home builders
Making burrows in banks along streams
But where they can't do this
They erect a large dam
Changing the landscape
In the way that Man can

They chomp through trees
With their teeth and their jaws
Carrying branches and twigs
In their mouths and their claws.
In the water beyond
This hodgepodge of logs
Lies a protected pond
Where they build a fine home
Which is known as a lodge

This lodge is shaped like a dome
To enter the beaver dives deep
Here he can keep his family safe ...
In a home to live in and sleep

LOG CABIN

HEAT RETREAT

Toads and frogs are am-phi-bians
Have you heard this word?
They begin their life in water
As eggs which grow legs
Becoming wriggling tadpoles

Tadpoles slowly change
And when they're big enough
They come out onto land
Where life can be quite tough

Keeping cool is the rule
So they need to own a home
Burrows near the water
Make perfect hidey-holes!

Tree frogs are tiny
As you would expect
They make their homes in leaves
Where they're not easy to detect
Some have color-changing camo
Which is like a built-in ammo
Designed to protect

TREEHUGGER!

21

ON THE MOVE

The hermit crab doesn't own his own home
I guess you could say he rents one
He finds an empty shell
That fits him fairly well
And carries it around
As a home where he can dwell

But it isn't very long
Before this home's outgrown
And he needs to get himself one bigger
He tries several on for size
Until he's found one that applies
Seems a wandering way to live, go figure!

A snail is a mollusc
A "what?!" did you say
It has a coiled shell
On its back
There it will squeeze
Taking its ease
Safe through the day
From attack

Snails hardly can see
Don't have noses to smell
Special cells in their feelers
Find them food very well

MOBILE HOME

These birds like to live in large colonies
The male birds weave many a nest
Working hard, using twigs, reeds and grasses
Not pausing in daylight to rest.
The female will line it with feathers and grass
When she's chosen the one she likes best

The male weavers are wonderful builders
Each nest has a perfect round door
Many nests hang down from the branches
Birds bustling in busy uproar
With water and food close to hand
Do these families need anything more?

KNOCK!
KNOCK!

It's a beautiful bird, the Blue Heron
Fish is its favorite dish
Its nest is always near water
Made of sticks, in a tree,
To raise chicks

Heron babies are fed by both parents
Who bring all kinds of food to the nest
Little herons are noisy and hungry
And give their poor parents no rest!

STICKS, NOT BRICKS

No skeleton has the octopus
Which means he's easy prey
But he has all kinds of tricks
To keep predators away

He can squeeze his squishy body
Into tiny little cracks
He can hide inside a shell
For the armor which he lacks

Our eight-legged friend
Likes to be left alone
He builds a sort of fortress
Made of shells, around his home

PRIVATE PROPERTY

PEEKING ...

Does an eel have a home?
Does he like to live alone?

Yes, an eel does have a home
It's a hole that's called a pit
Inside a rock or hollow stone
He likes to hide away in it

This pair of eels seem to share
A homely hole most happily
Lurking low inside their lair
To pounce on passing prey they see

ROOM FOR ONE!

Peeping from crevices etched in the coral
Hiding in hollows carved into the rocks
Gliding and sliding
All kinds of fish
Make homes inside holes
Through which they can swish

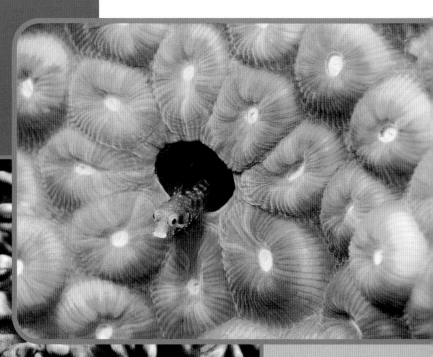

PYTHON

WOLVERINE

SPIDER

SQUIRREL

WOODPECKERS

SKUNK ANEMONE FISH

MEERKAT

LOBSTER

LIZARD

GECKO

INDEX

Amphibians, 20, 21

Ants, 9

Bats, 14

Beavers, 19

Birds, 24, 25, 30

Crabs, 2, 22, 32

Crustaceans, 2, 22, 31, 32

Eels, 27

Elephants, 16

Fish, 4, 28, 29, 31

Frogs, 20, 21

Geckos, 31

Insects, 6, 7, 9, 10

Lizards, 31

Lobsters, 31

Mammals, 1, 3, 5, 11-17, 19, 30-32

Meerkats, 31

Moles, 13

Molluscs, 23, 26

Mongooses, 11

Mice, 15

Octopuses, 26

Opossums, 32

Prairie dogs, 5, 12

Pythons, 30

Raccoons, 32

Reptiles, 18, 23, 31, 32

Skunk anemone fish, 31

Snails, 23

Snakes, 30

Spiders, 8, 30, 32

Spittlebugs, 7

Squirrels, 30

Termites, 10

Toads, 20

Tortoises, 18

Turtles, 18

Warthogs, 1, 3, 17

Wasps, 6

Wolverines, 30

Woodpeckers, 30

ACKNOWLEDGMENTS

Photography by: Samuel Acosta, Dean Bertoncelj, Davit Buachidze, Steve Byland, Katarina Christenson, Gerrit de Vries, Boyan Dimitrov, Dennis Donohue, Anatoli Dubkov, EcoPrint, Dan Exton, Faup, Alan Gleichman, Gorshkov25, ShannonGraeme, Arto Hakola, Eric Isselée, Natalie Jean, Hans Christoph Kappel/npl/Minden Pictures, Jason Kasumovic, Eduard Kyslynskyy, Hugh Lansdown, Brian Lasenby, Peter Leahy, Ali Mufti, Jaana Piira, Pi-Lens, Pix2go, Luiz A. Rocha, Serg64, Shutterstock Images, Igor Sirbu, Jackie Smithson, Mike Tan, Mogens Trolle, Wiltshireyeoman, Frank B Yuwono, Peter Waters, Keith Wheatley, and Rick Wylie.

Gratitude is also extended to Alaska Pacific University (Marine Biology program), Australian Museum, www.britannica.com, Defenders of Wildlife, Carole Dennis, National Geographic, and San Diego Zoo.

TARANTULA

OPOSSUM

RACCOON